21 thoughts; 21 truths

Anvika Pande

Presentation by *BookLeaf Publishing*

Web: www.bookleafpub.com

E-mail: info@bookleafpub.com

ISBN: 9789358318739

First edition 2024

To courage and what we do in its desperate absence.

Also to my parents.

I don't fear god as much as I fear my mother

I don't fear god as much as I fear my mother,
because I've stopped sleeping past 9.
No other other voice scatters my unholy spirit,
though she says it's god who will keep me
checked in line .

Yet when I clean my room from its depressing
mess,
I don't open the door to a holy being,
I call her loudly to the sight of my new found
belief,
her maternal pride and my self-declared healing.

And if I cut my hair a strand too short,
I dont worry if my divinity will fade,
I worry if she'll think the length is still pretty,
I worry if she'll think I've made a mistake

And when I win an award, certificates, trophies,
galore,
I don't count them in faith of a higher power.
I dust them off on the mantel in her living room,
so she can glance at them in her sanctified hour

And when I inevitably chance my moral
compass,
I have no fear of what god will say,
instead I cringe at this reaching my mother,
her verdict I'd less prefer than judgment day.

And when I close my eyes and pray to god,
I am not greeted by a heavily bearded face,
Instead I hear a familiar voice yelling,
"It's past 9, you're going to be late".

Thank God For Friendship, Thank God For You

Ease the speed of time,
calming without a bruise.
Feed my gentle thoughts
and let the echt boom.

Hug the force of my
many awkward verities,
and lend me some of your's
so we may breathe in certainty.

In credence and fair
do I feel
when I sense harbinger of yours.
No malocchio
will I ever intended;
no resentment or unkempt scores.

Unfold me with grace,
embracing; insecurity withdrew.
Wipe my tears, no haste,
I owe myself to you.

(for sanju)

A room and a hallway

The question stands confused,
it begs me to enter this new room.
Yet I am face to face with the thought of four
ways
and continue to remain in my familiar hallway.

If I am to curl this novel knob,
all my slamming fears may be hatched to a stop.
This dreadful hinge could greet the picturesque,
I could be invited by new pillows, better sleep
and a shiny desk.

But I'm sleeping just fine now,
and what if the room makes weird sounds?
What if the floor comes scratched,
and with it my comfortability, detached?

Not to mention, the hallway is an old friend.
One I have known in life and in time again.
You can't just leave an old friend behind,
that would be leaving a latched lock lost, a
longing confined.

But the walls of the hall pull me in closer,

warp my placid dreams with a time ticking tide
over.
They mock me with endless corridors of regret,
and haunt me with shadows of darkening
silhouettes.

And there stands the taunting tear of the new
door,
It's leaking slit glowing from its roof till it's
floor.
Yet this seeming light may paint planks for a
betraying service.
Will it lend new grief or give old hope a chance
to resurface?

On how much borrowed time will I seethe from
pretend
that I am truly content with where I am.
The question corners my decision into effect,
but I sojourn in my suspicions, still stuck, still
kept.

If and when

6

But if we stop talking
And my eyes meet yours
Let it be the last taste of my youth
I ever wondered for.

And when we drift apart
And leave our souls sore
I'll have our many moonlight memories
Where my heart was only ever yours.

Untitled

A generous crooked finger
in the breadth of my growing hair
that you once stopped braiding.

A willful crooked finger
in the clumps of a child's yogurt
that you once stopped feeding.

The morning now;
ever so desperate
for the faint of your singing voice
and a daughter
for her crumbling green.

Was this called to a halt
when my eyes met yours,
speaking words you did not teach,
or for perishing sights,
neither of us wished I'd witnessed.

Forgiven and forgotten so (as it always is),
come back and soothe me to sleep.
Come back and let me face another day,
this time,
closer to your motherhood.

The pressure of the "perfect goodbye"

The pressure of the "perfect goodbye"
                an act of pretend.
Where somber hearts lay unprevailed,
and reality fails to win.

Anxious eyes
          unto
              unbecoming smiles
and sounds of hollow laughter.
Swallowed tears
from the loneliness of fear,
and inadequate solace thereafter.

Increased banter with intrusive thoughts:
          struggling and suppressed.
A warning to the imagination
to not skip 30 minutes ahead.

Desolate avails of empty embraces,
prickingly provident and cold
A continuously painful game of charade
which will always and inevitably unfold.

I miss my friends

Promise me,
that when we meet,
despite the year's gone by
you will still call my name
as loudly as you did in our school's hall;
always as you did,
despite the bitterness of the morning light.

And I promise to you,
I'll rush
as eagerly as I always did
in the sweetness of the morning light.

Consider these my glory days,
when I did not know the
laughter
a corridor could hold,
or the disappointment
I would carry
when the back of the classroom wasn't invited
by you.

I found the answer to life!

What do I owe,
to this anxious pleasure,
of a glimpse that is not mine,
and voice's of quaint blether.

Still, linger keeps,
nestled in my heaped notions,
till I am damp,
yet in the light of dooming weeps .

An analogue to their sanity,
do I etch,
pleasantries of pretend.
Of a half-masked grin
brought till dawn
greets you again.

Though its ebb and flow
call resonance
to the many sounds of life;
might the ease hide
in nonchalance,
the hope of seeking
emptiness,
in it, we confide.

New friends and apparently a new plot

Inexhaustible screenplays
I've written to you
in hopes of your approval.
With script that has
the same few actors,
but to me you seem too frugal.

I've seen you give
my deepest wish
to others less deserving.
You can change the light, the plot, the stage
but please!
keep the characters enduring.

Have I failed a test
of companionship,
unbeknown to me?
I've shown my efforts
in your stage directions,
and proved my loyalties.

Remove the narrator, add a Greek chorus
and fluctuate the theme.
But all I ask, is that you don't

write an ending soliloquy.

The dialogues seem now
of certain waste
and futility.
If all my life was on a stage,
it would be a true tragedy!

Redemption

In the gentle solitude of a dusked beam
can hope be promised within the hour;
the early faith of a reminisced tune,
a callusing charm, a moment fleeting with
power.

Still, efforts cannot seek in lost absolutions,
of grief, of failed suffering.
Only a foolish swear would rhyme of reaped
rewards
in barren minutes doused with futile roughening.

Dishonesties may swell in our ripples of
deserving,
of entitled lochs, a grabbing surge to claim.
Yet pith might curl in a wave not emerging,
in the clam of a sea, permissed, limpid, and
unblamed.

Under timeless crests of swollen eyes
might the looming sight of confession unveil.
Might we hope to find the ken of redemption,
in ourselves, truly then it must prevail.

If this is how I break

If this is how I break,
I'd let my mother's arms hold me,
I'd let the ache pass by
as though untouched by the world, I'm still holy.

With each breath I'd pray
and match my rhythm with her's.
Each shatter of mine, a sigh
Oh! relentless remorse.

And if my soul did crack,
and the earth fell apart,
I'd thank the gleaming stars
that I had fallen in your arms.

I can't decide a title

Crushing in the darkest hour
hopeful jests with guilt.
A kindness not of mine,
foriegn feeling of the skin.

Thoughts crying aught,
begging of my unbelonging.
Bleed the night pitch ink
of a poet's painful longing

Stitch the broken honours
sworn by a bullish self.
Humbled to a thread,
vexed from perfections of the twelfth.

Doomed in all the choice,
perplexed and amused in result.
If I am who I say I am,
leaving wouldn't claim the difficult.

papa's stories

To run with you when my legs get old
and crumple beneath my weight.
I wish to chronicle the same few stories,
I've been repeating for half a decade.

The generous yarn of my stripling primes
an etch of youth and yearning.
A chance to clasp my buried self,
revived hope, betrayal and learning,

Alas, my soul, as humane as I,
did I have courage only the regretful crave.
This strive which mourned my childhood field,
and kinship that I covet to this day.

In eluctability, I found myself,
straining, stumbling and small.
Yet, this is how to rejoice in self,
crave redemption, only if you fall.

And in the gruel of many finite days,
when hope begins to fail,
take life with humor, a bit of earth
and gratitude of the day.

I charm my plenty hardships now,
for lost fear of the grave.
Now, a smile simply from the two of you,
is ample enough to sustain.

I'll run with you till my memories eventually
fade.
I'll run with you, till you outrun me,
I promise, when I was your age,
I too, was nothing but afraid.

Barefoot amongst boyhood

When the leaves burn autumn,
and the turtle dove's tale unfolds,
say that we will still watch the shedding sun
and let it call to our friendship.

And even in the gruelling years to come by,
we will glimpse the sound of our quandom
smiles,
veiled under the colours
of the seventh heaven sky.

Though weakness may shackle our crows feet,
we will upturn the torn topaz fields,
and aid water to our drying leaves.
Aligning truth with our comradery.

As placid as our inner bairn may be,
say that we will continue to race
as fast as the wind
and let it twirl the straight of our hair.
Barefoot amongst boyhood may we become
anew again.

Wasted Time

It starts in a classroom
with a teacher droning on
so you stare at the clock
until time moves on.

It happens with an early bus,
and you, a moment too late.
So you walk till the next stop
because a moment can never simply go to waste.

Sometimes it's a mistake,
you've made a decision belated.
A deadline missed.
A procrastination abyss.

So you beat yourself up,
and swear it was a one time thing.
An internal promise.
Beg to Cronos, swear you're honest.

Inevitably it happens again
and again and again and again,
and you can't understand
how you've failed to comply to your own
command.

At last it occurs,
you're royally disarranged.
A task you've disgraced.
Absolutely nothing to save face.

So you try your best
to make the most of your mess.
Though the thought repeated and futile,
you've caused a decent plethora of otherwhile.

You can't seem to fight the guilt
of all the minutes you've forced still.
All the chances that could have been,
yet here you are, at the start again

"Its okay"
you tell (delusion) yourself,
it's an event with purpose.
Life moves on,
a little bit of wasted time definitely can't hurt us.

A poem about my sister

My sister told me to write a poem for her,
but I dont know how to begin.
How do I write about you my dear,
a poem for my most beloved kin?

It is an affinity much too complex,
one which flows through soul and time.
No wire of words could wield a verse that wise,
no symphony left for me to rhyme.

How do I write about the one which grows with
you,
with plaits in our hair and the whole world new.
With words shot so deep, only eachother know,
yet its always you I dial when faced to a phone

Its been 8 years too long since we have shared a
roof
a distance so deep, yet never undoing our roots.
With months that pass amidst unshared meals
every lunch I have, I save you the last piece.

So call our shared name, in solidarity, in pain,
and I will follow along blindly.
I carry you in my core, inevitably unchanged

a sisterhood so kind, oh it's just so strange!

You have put me under a lot of pressure,
as older sisters tend to do,
so this is my final attempt,
this is my poem about you.

My friend's rooftop

To the rooftop,
        which I gave many midnights
        and carefully closed doors.

Its creaking slates,
and daring corners
on which we sat
and lived indefinitely
in the union of our
Insatiable youth.

        To you I owe,
            the price of a sky
filled with three stars,
            and the memories
of teenagehood.

moment(s)

The moment of shared laughter
and rediscovered purpose
is when I become
painstakingly aware of the
Distance life has forced between us.

In the moment that follows
we childishly avoid
the deafening silence,
in which I try to fight the guilt of choice
and you,
with anguished futility,
blame yourself.

Both angry and insignificant,
in the audacious face of time,
while the moment passes,
fleetingly unappreciated.

Three rings and a new town

There I sat, the room blotched in red,
each brushstroke, a search for my name.
It seeped and soaked and tried to stay,
till I was wet and painted astray.

And the woman waved her placid hand
in a brag of Georgian architecture.
Her gleaming fist, a bit too proud
for what her town's average achievements were.

And as she spoke, paraded rather,
I caught sight of a peculiar scene.
Three rings were stacked on her fourth finger,
two sights which I'd never once seen.

The rings glamoured each narrowing cinch,
graying in silver and custom ways.
Each ream, a bore, echoing her wince,
each jewel gleaming with faux grace.

And every woman I saw for the next two weeks
was branded with self the same.
A hankering hope of idiosyncrasy,
yet their pledged hand could be easily replaced.

Their annular daze, balefully gliding,
surrendering a will once more.
Carving body with metallic portraiture,
It's whipping rim, ready to implore.

And the rings glared at my stifling cries,
mocking me with similar fate.
The gleaming prize, a barricade too tight,
I couldn't move, I was drowned in paint.

Young Faith

Even when
my faith was new
and I still yearned aught,
I was followed by
It's temporary relief
and my forbearing distraught.

Though my feet grazed
    grass and celestial
and my fingers on
my fathers hyacinth;
My chest bud
in infinite ache
of my dichotomy in innocence.

Perhaps if I
    held her face
a minute more longer,
She could have lived
a child guilt-free
like the dusk held sky
or an angel glimpsed flower.

A poem about courage

In times uncertain where bitter
anchors peace of mind.
Seek in self, an almond hull
and in it, hope will crave to be defined.

With all its poise it will give succor
through nights which made you fragile.
It will lend to you a potent sustenance,
with force that strains the futile.

And when time stands still with sliced thin light
depth will hone many hurts.
But bear past truths, in ebb of patience,
you will find yourself rediscovered.

And until you greet Courage
to branch your bough and parch your flowering
thirst,
place faith that even the smallest bud
can make the soul return.